SCIENTIFIC AMERICAN | EDUCATIONAL PUBLISHING

SCIENTIFIC AMERICAN INVESTIGATES FOSSILS

HUMAN FOSSILS

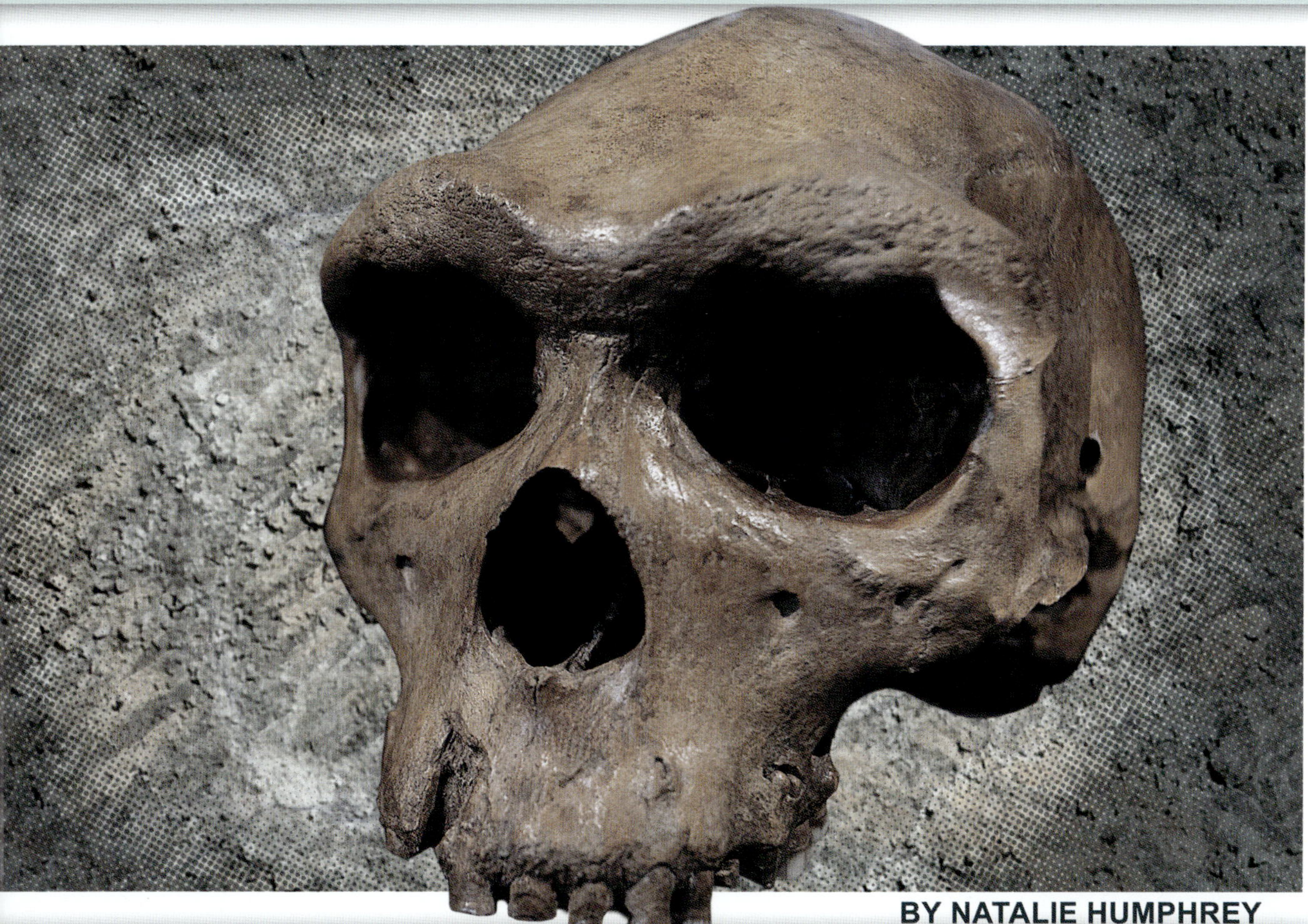

BY NATALIE HUMPHREY

Published in 2025 by The Rosen Publishing Group
in association with Scientific American Educational Publishing
2544 Clinton Street, Buffalo NY 14224

Cataloging-in-Publication Data
Names: Humphrey, Natalie.
Title: Human fossils / Natalie Humphrey.
Description: New York : Scientific American Educational Publishing, an imprint of Rosen Publishing, 2025. | Series: Scientific American investigates fossils | Includes glossary and index.
Identifiers: ISBN 9781725351981 (pbk.) | ISBN 9781725351998 (library bound) | ISBN 9781725352001 (ebook)
Subjects: LCSH: Fossil hominids–Juvenile literature.
Classification: LCC GN282.H86 2025 | DDC 569.9–dc23

Portions of this work were originally authored by Kathleen Connors and published as *Human Fossils*. All new material in this edition is authored by Natalie Humphrey.

Designer: Andrea Davison-Bartolotta
Editor: Natalie Humphrey

Photo credits: Cover, p. 1 (main) Roberto Nistri/Alamy Stock Photo; cover, p. 1 (dirt texture) komkrit Preechachanwate/Shutterstock.com; cover, p. 1 (stone texture) Efefne Design/Shutterstock.com; cover, p. 1 (vingette) Yurlick/Shutterstock.com; p. 5 (inset) photobar/Shutterstock.com; p. 5 (main) Xolodan/Shutterstock.com; p. 7 PTZ Pictures/Shutterstock.com; p. 9 Jononmac46/File:Gibraltar Skull (1).JPG/Wikimedia Commons; p. 11 (inset) Josep Curto/Shutterstock.com; p. 11 (main) WH_Pics/Shutterstock.com; p. 13 Svet foto/Shutterstock.com; p. 15 Sailko/File:Resti di ardipithecus ramidus detto ardi, da aramis (afar), 4,4 milioni di anni fa 02.jpg/Wikimedia Commons; p. 16 File:TPL2 human fossil remains.TIF/Wikimedia Commons; p. 17 David Herraez Calzada/Shutterstock.com; p. 18 one line plot/Shutterstock.com; p. 19 (left) Lapis2380/Shutterstock.com; p. 19 (right) Faviel_Raven/Shutterstock.com; p. 21 Puwadol Jaturawutthichai/Shutterstock.com.s

Printed in the United States of America

CPSIA compliance information: Batch #CWSA25. For Further Information contact Rosen Publishing at 1-800-237-9932.

CONTENTS

Words in the glossary appear in **bold** type the first time they are used in the text.

HOW TO STUDY HUMANS

Paleontologists are scientists who study **fossils** to learn what the ancient world may have looked like. But there's another kind of paleontologist with a big name and an even bigger job! Paleoanthropologists study the world of ancient humans by looking at human and humanoid fossils.

In the 1800s, scientist Charles Darwin wrote a book connecting the ancient **ancestors** of humans to that of apes. Today, scientists still believe humans and apes are linked, but we know a lot more about these ancient humans!

Something humanoid is a living thing that looks and acts like a human.

BECOMING A FOSSIL

Fossils form over a long period of time. The living parts of bones break down. What's left behind are the nonliving parts of the bone. Sometimes, **minerals** fill the pores, or small holes, in the bones. Other times, the minerals replace the bones entirely.

To study ancient humans, paleoanthropologists look at the fossils from human **skeletons**. Scientists usually find only a piece of a skeleton or part of a bone. Complete skeletons are so special, they usually get names!

FUN FACT

THE OLDEST AND MOST COMPLETE FOSSIL FROM AN ANCIENT HUMAN, A SKELETON NAMED LITTLE FOOT, IS AROUND 3.67 MILLION YEARS OLD.

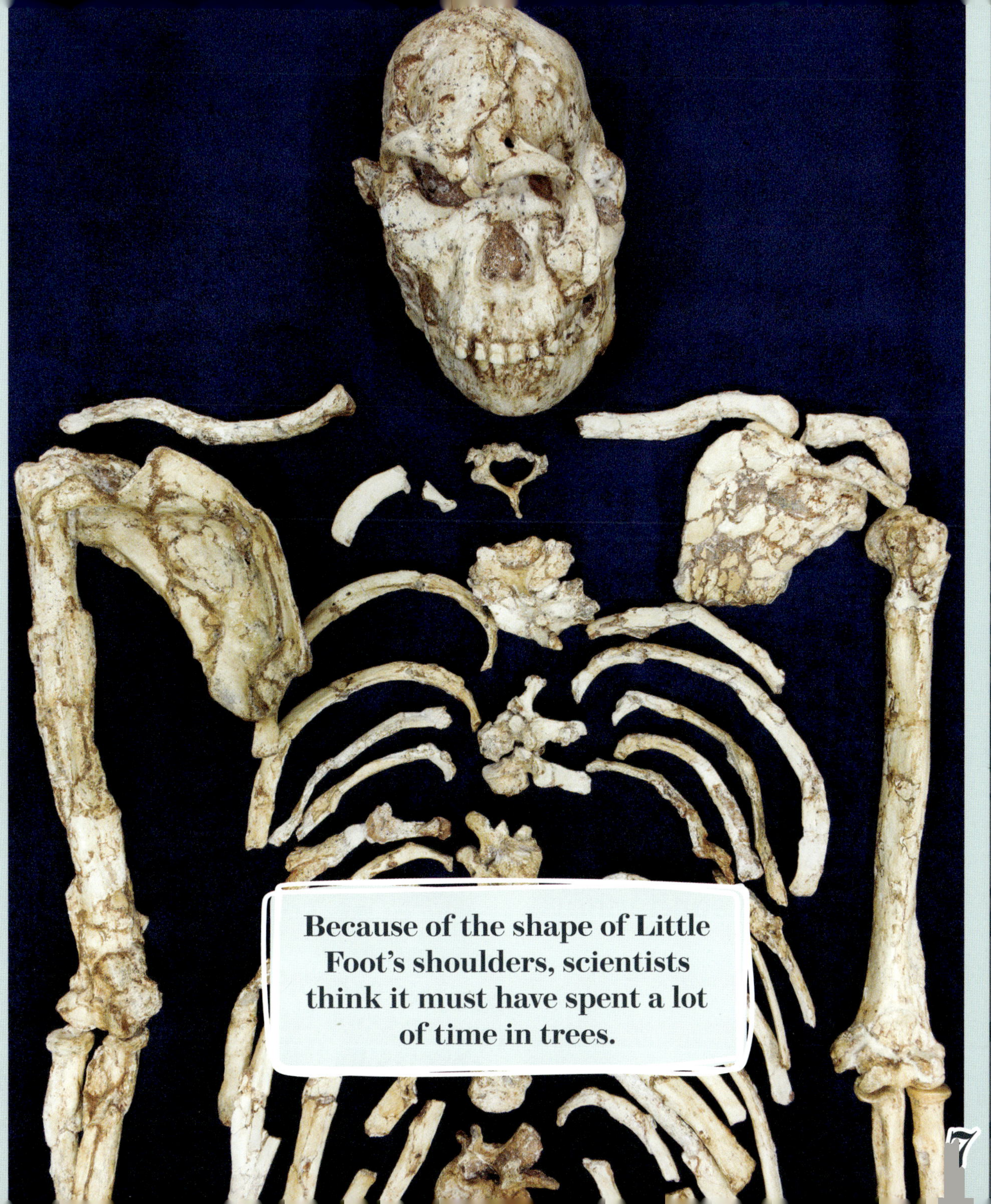

Because of the shape of Little Foot's shoulders, scientists think it must have spent a lot of time in trees.

FINDING FOSSILS

In 1848, a British military officer found a **skull** in Gibraltar at the southern tip of Spain. But no one knew what kind of skull they found! In 1857, German miners found parts of a skull scientists believed were from the same species, or kind.

Scientists discovered more of these fossils in Belgium in 1886. Scientists later decided these fossils were from a group of very early humans, which they called Neanderthals.

FUN FACT

EUGÈNE DUBOIS UNCOVERED THE FIRST FOSSILS OF ANOTHER HUMAN SPECIES IN INDONESIA. DUBOIS NAMED THIS SPECIES *HOMO ERECTUS*.

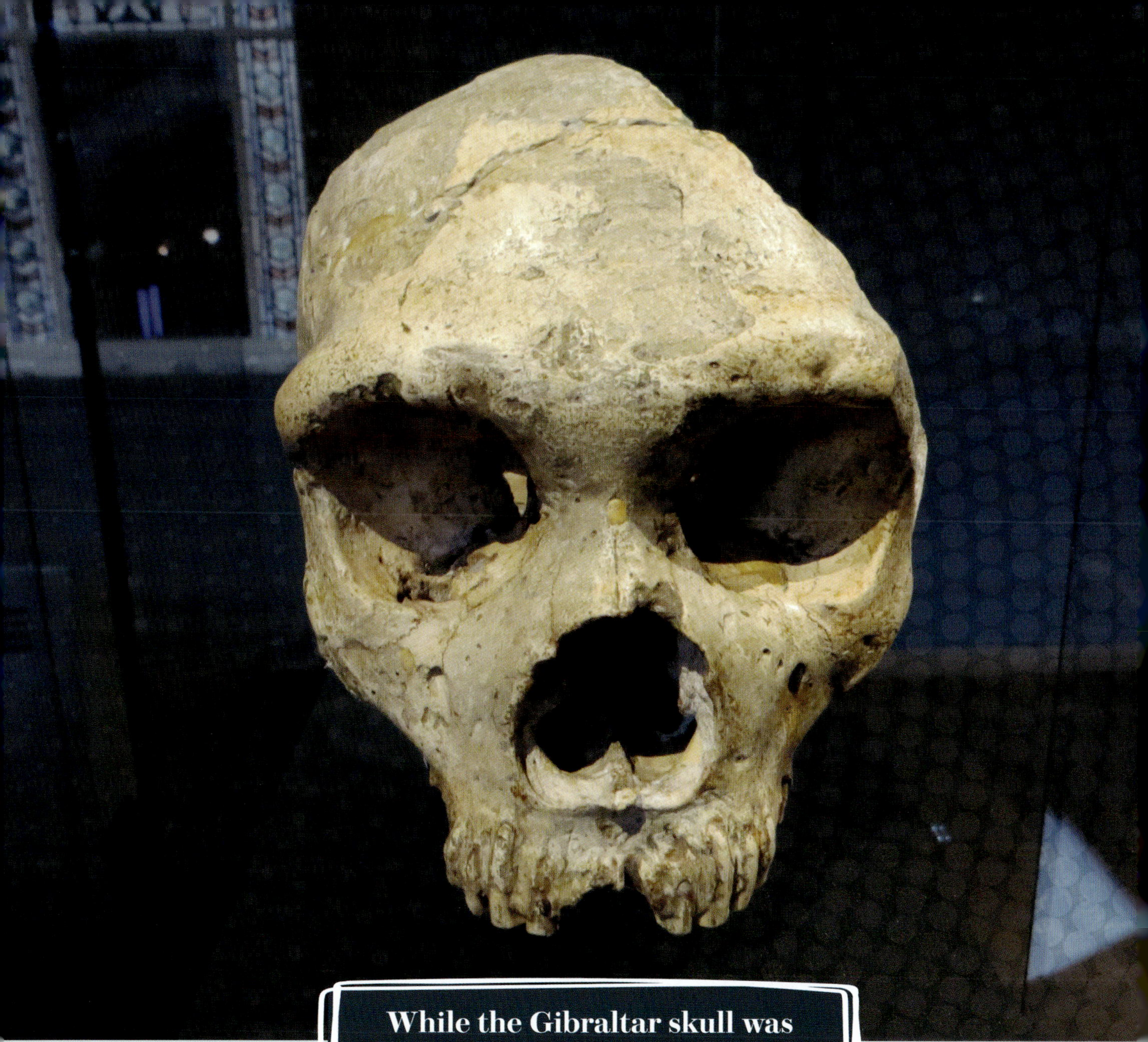

While the Gibraltar skull was found in 1848, scientists didn't find out what species it was until 1865.

HOMINIDAE

The family of animals that both humans and apes are part of is called Hominidae. The members of one group within this family are called hominins. These are human ancestors that have died out. Ancient hominin fossils show some human features and some ape features. Scientists don't always agree about the connection between these fossils, modern humans, and apes.

Paleoanthropologists have concluded that many human species and other hominins lived at the same time. Some of these species even lived in the same place!

Scientists have recorded more than 20 species of hominin.

FUN FACT

MODERN HUMANS ARE CALLED *HOMO SAPIENS*.

DATING FOSSILS

One of the oldest hominin fossils found dates back to about 7 million years ago. The oldest fossils of modern humans are between 100,000 and 200,000 years old.

There are a few ways for scientists to figure out how old a fossil is. Sometimes they will use superposition. This establishes the fossil's age based on the rock **layer** it's found in. Another way is **radiometric dating**. Radiometric dating can help **researchers** find out how old a fossil is more exactly.

Many of the earliest hominin fossils, such as this *Sahelanthropus tchadensis* skull, came from Africa.

FUN FACT

SUPERPOSITION IS THE PLACEMENT OF LAYERS OF ROCK ON TOP OF ONE ANOTHER. THE LOWER LAYERS ARE OLDER THAN THE HIGHER LAYERS.

SPECIAL DISCOVERIES

Scientists have recorded more than 6,000 hominin fossils. In 1974, an American paleoanthropologist found a 3.4-million-year-old fossilized skeleton in Ethiopia. Scientists named it Lucy. Lucy was the oldest and most complete human ancestor found at the time.

Another fossil nicknamed Ardi was found in Africa in 1992. In 2009, after many years of research, scientists first showed the 4.4-million-year-old skeleton to the public. Through these fossils, scientists learned more about how humans and apes are connected.

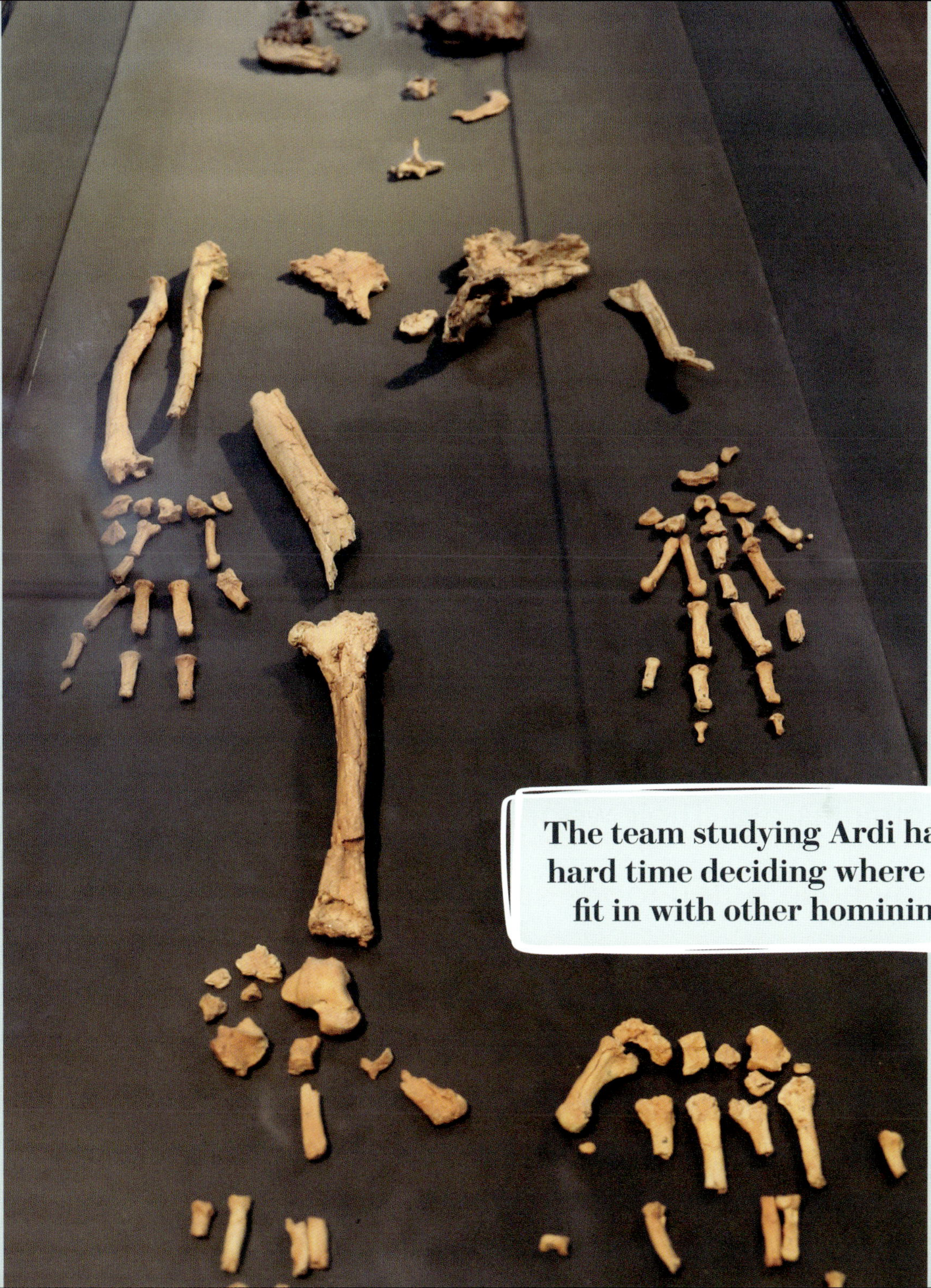

The team studying Ardi had a hard time deciding where she fit in with other hominins.

ALL ABOUT TEETH

One of the ways scientists can tell the difference between an early hominin skull and another primate is by looking at their teeth! Teeth like our teeth today came about very early in hominin **evolution**.

Scientists have learned a lot about early hominins by looking at their teeth! Fossilized teeth can show what hominins ate. Their wear patterns show that the group may have eaten foods such as plants, nuts, and small animals.

Paleoanthropologists have found more teeth than any other type of human fossil.

FUN FACT

BY STUDYING THE **PLAQUE** LEFT BEHIND ON ANCIENT TEETH, SCIENTISTS LEARNED MORE ABOUT WHAT HOMININS ATE! SCIENTISTS FOUND TINY FOSSILS OF FISH SCALES, FLESH, AND MORE ON FOSSILIZED HUMAN TEETH.

WALKING OR CLIMBING?

By looking at fossilized leg, hand, or **pelvis** bones, paleoanthropologists learned that ancient hominins may not have moved like us. Modern humans walk on two feet, but ancient hominins used their hands and feet to move through trees.

The shape of these bones shows how hominins and early humans moved around. Scientists can't agree on whether our ancestors walked like apes by using their **knuckles** at some point in time.

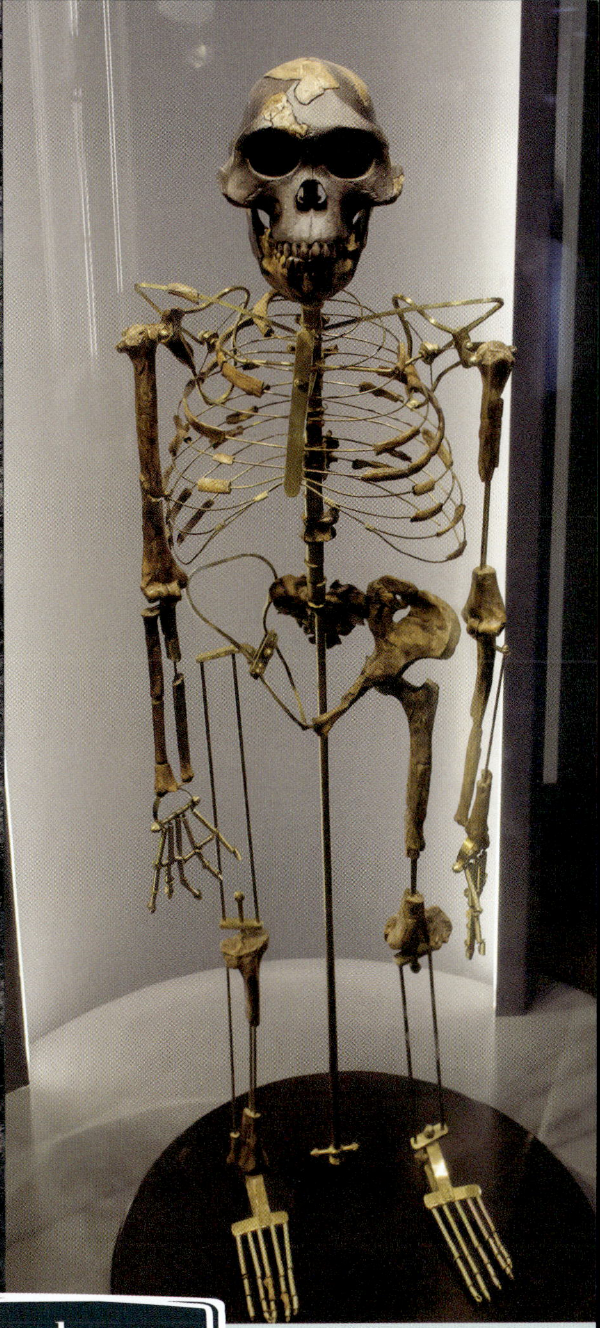

Early humans may have started walking on two feet around 6 million years ago.

FINDING MORE

While many ancient hominins have been discovered, scientists still have more questions about what these ancient humans were like. Each fossil is carefully studied and cared for, but it can take years for researchers to learn which member of the Hominidae family a skull is from.

Scientists are also changing what they believe ancient humans may have looked like. With so many discoveries to make, there's always something new to find about ancient humans!

The Human Family Tree

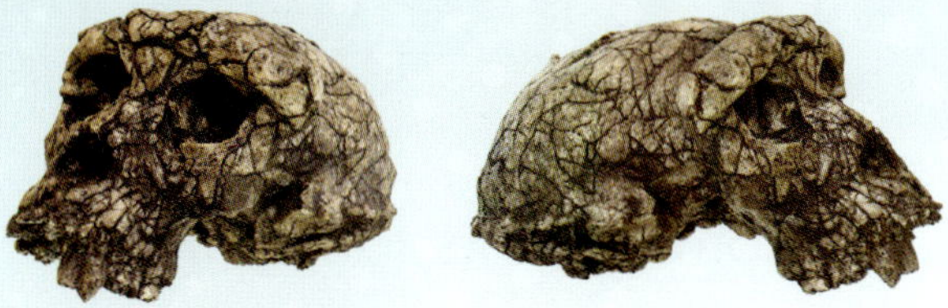

Sahelanthropus tchadensis
dated to 7-6 million years ago

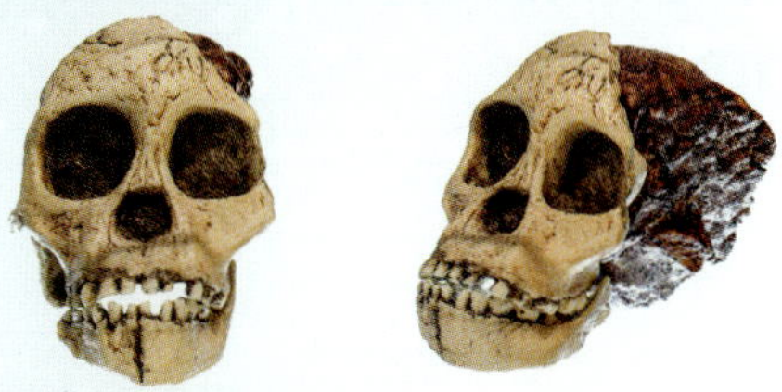

Australopithecus africanus
dated to 2,500,000 years ago

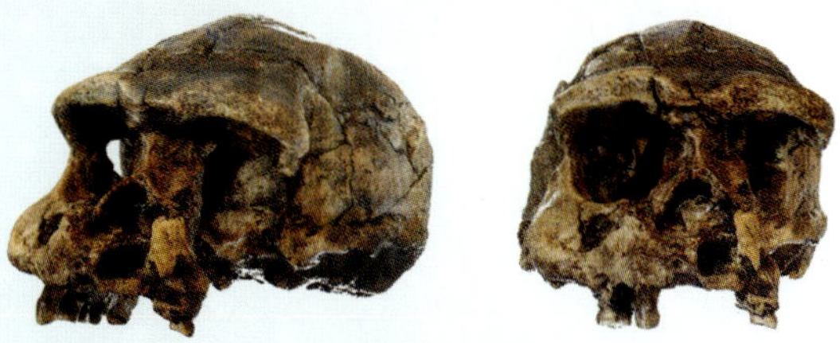

Homo erectus
dated to 1,000,000 years ago

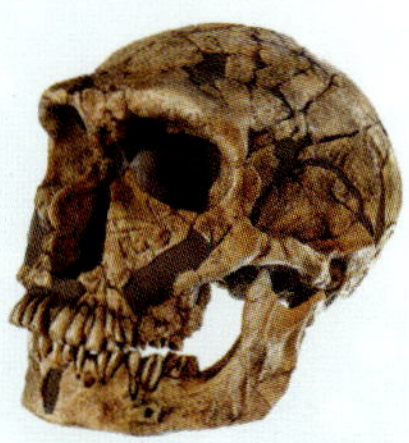

Homo neanderthalensis
dated to 50,000 years ago

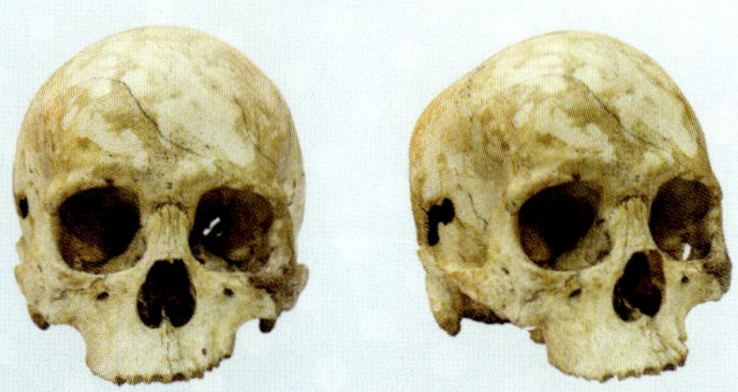

Homo sapiens
dated to 30,000-10,000 years ago

GLOSSARY

ancestor: An animal that lived before others in its family tree.

evolution: The process of animals and plants slowly changing into new forms over thousands of years.

fossil: The marks or remains of plants and animals that formed over thousands or millions of years.

knuckle: The joint that joins the fingers to the hand.

layer: One thickness of something lying over or under another.

mineral: Matter in the ground that forms rocks.

pelvis: A large bone in an animal's body where the legs and spine connect.

plaque: A white, soft material that forms on teeth and may cause bacteria to grow.

radiometric dating: A method of finding out how old something is

researcher: A person who studies something to find something new.

skeleton: The bony frame of the body.

skull: The bony frame of the head and face.

FOR MORE INFORMATION

Books

Amin, Anita Nahta. *Dig and Discover Fossils.* Oxford, UK: Raintree, 2024.

Holmes, Kirsty. *People: Exploring the Civilizations of Humans from Long Ago*. New York, NY: Gareth Stevens Publishing, 2022.

Websites

American Museum of Natural History: Anthropology
www.amnh.org/explore/ology/anthropology
Learn more about ancient humans and how scientists study them.

Smithsonian 3D Digitization: Hominin Fossils
https://3d.si.edu/collections/hominin-fossils
Explore 3D versions of the Smithsonian National Museum of Natural History's collection of hominin fossils.

INDEX